101 Uses *for an* Old Farm Tractor

RAINCOAST BOOKS

Vancouver

First published in Canada in 2000 by
Raincoast Books
9050 Shaughnessy Street
Vancouver, B.C. V6P 6E5
(604) 323-7100
www.raincoast.com

Published by Voyageur Press, Inc., Stillwater, MN 55082 U.S.A.

Canadian Cataloguing in Publication Data
Main entry under title:
   101 uses for an old farm tractor

   ISBN 1-55192-442-0
   1. Farm tractors—Humor. 2. Canadian wit and humor (English)* 3. Canadian wit and humor, Pictorial. I. Title: One hundred one uses for an old farm tractor.
PN6231.F36O52 2000   631.3'72'0207
C00-911043-7

00   01   02   03   04   5   4   3   2   1

Edited by Michael Dregni
Designed by Kristy Tucker
Printed in Hong Kong

On the endpapers: A Twin City tractor and its faithful crew.
On the frontipiece: Everyone was excited by the arrival of the family's new Massey-Harris tractor, as pictured on this 1950s Massey *Buyer's Guide*.
On the title pages: A 1930s Oliver 70 Row Crop advertising painting by M. E. Swenson.
On the acknowledgments page: A happy farm family with their Minneapolis-Moline U tractor. (Minnesota Historical Society)

Acknowledgments

Our thanks to all who helped make this book come to life: John O. Allen of J. C. Allen & Son; Keith Baum; Ken Gianini of the Minnesota State Fair; Jerry Irwin; Andy Kraushaar; Andrew Morland; Robert N. Pripps; Paul Rezendes; Les Stegh of Deere & Company; and everyone at Voyageur Press who helped dream up uses for old tractors.

101 Uses for an Old Farm Tractor

The glories of the farming life, from
a 1920s Case brochure.

Baby Buggy

A budding young tractor driver checks out the ergonomics of the latest John Deere at the Minnesota State Fair in the 1960s.

1

After a hard day working in the field, a youngster catches a few winks in his homemade John Deere Model B wagon. (Photograph © Jerry Irwin)

Walker

If you're going to be a farmer, you better learn to drive tractor as early as possible. (Photograph © Andy Kraushaar)

3

How long you been driving tractor? A young farmer pilots his Massey-Ferguson 330 pedal tractor, pulling a miniature utility wagon carrying his younger brother. (Photograph © Jerry Irwin)

4

Dream Machine

Like grandfather, like grandson. Allen Martin sits on his 1935 John Deere Model B while his grandson, Jonathan Martin, pilots a Model 60 pedal tractor. (Photograph © Keith Baum)

If you can't get them off their favorite Allis-Chalmers, you might as well put the situation to good use. (Library of Congress)

Merry-Go-Round

The Short Turn 20/30 tractor of 1916–1918 could turn around within its own track at the end of a row. It was the brainchild of inventor John Dahl and was built in both Bemidji and Minneapolis, Minnesota.

The balance of components on this pioneering motor grader make it look
as though it could have served as a precarious see-saw on weekends
after it was finishing grading roads.

8

Jungle Gym

A threshing crew takes a break from their work—or play?—with their steam traction engine near Stillwater, Minnesota, in 1931.

Driver's Education Vehicle

A youngster steers the family's Farmall Cub—with the reassuring presence
of Dad sitting behind him should anything go awry.
(Photograph © Jerry Irwin)

For Making a Boy Feel Like a Man

This threshing-bee veteran takes a breather from his work stoking the firebox of his crew's Advance-Rumely steamer. (Photograph © Jerry Irwin)

Sunday Drive

The Johnny Popper was the ideal vehicle for a Sunday drive—but everyone came rushing home when the dinner bell rang. Artist Walter Haskell Hinton's painting captured the farmwife's call to the table in an image that appeared in a classic John Deere calendar. (Deere & Company)

Farmer Harry Wood and family stand proudly in front of their Minneapolis-Moline UDLX Comfortractor in 1938. M-M marketed the
U-Deluxe as a tractor for the whole family: It could plow fields during
the week and then be driven to church on Sunday.
(Minnesota Historical Society)

Family Vacation Vehicle

Pack up your troubles and get away from it all! The Joliet Tractor
Company's "half-track" machine of the 1910s could take you
anywhere you wanted to go.

The whole gang gathers around its Ford NAA Golden Jubilee tractor and makes it feel part of the family.

Show and Tell

The family's Minneapolis-Moline UDLX Comfortractor was always the hit of show and tell at school—and in the days before the fad of crowding into telephone booths, you could always see how many friends fit into the U-Deluxe's novel new cab! (Minnesota Historical Society)

Charles Atlas Muscle Builder

Building muscles the hard way, a youth cranks over the engine on his family's Case tractor in the days before starter motors became common accessories. (Photograph © J. C. Allen & Son)

17

Women's Liberator

Tractors—such as this Minneapolis-Moline Z—gave farm women power.

18

Tractors were often a first car for farm youths—although they were rarely
allowed to drive the machines far from the fields that needed plowing.
(Photograph © J. C. Allen & Son)

For the Rebel Without a Cause

When your parents wouldn't allow you to buy a motor-cycle, the family's Fordson Major had to substitute as a ride with attitude. Just remember: Even James Dean grew up on a farm.

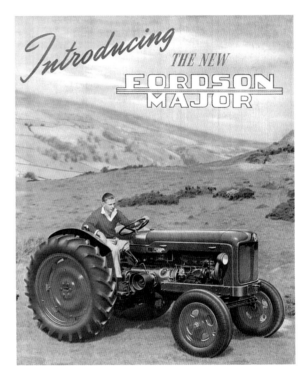

Introducing THE NEW **FORDSON MAJOR**

"Minnie Moline" was the pin-up of choice for tractor-smitten farm youths everywhere. Here, she poses on a 1939 Minneapolis-Moline UDLX, although without its famous enclosed cab. (Minnesota Historical Society)

Pick Up Girls

The latest Massey-Harris was the ideal machine to catch the eye of that certain special lady.

No man could resist a Johnny Popper. This painting by artist Walter Haskell Hinton pictured the men going off to World War II while the women took over in the fields. (Deere & Company)

Hot Date

Few dates were as romantic as a trip to the local fair's Machinery Hill to check out the latest and greatest in tractors.
(Minnesota State Fair collection)

24

If you played your cards right with your Waterloo Boy–Overtime tractor, romance could blossom—and you could get some needed plowing done at the same time.

Honeymoon Vehicle

A homemade "Doodle Bug" was the perfect "starter tractor" for a young couple setting off on their new married life together. (Glenbow Archives)

26

Recreational Vehicle

With the day's work done, the Massey-Harris was the ideal vehicle to get
you to the old fishing hole in a flash.

Convertible

Chic Cadillac rag-tops and convertible '57 Chevys had nothing on tractors when it came to top-down motoring. Kenneth Anderson's 1940s John Deere Model H could also double as a beach hut or lifeguard stand. (Photograph © Andrew Morland)

Beach Hut

Fishing Guide

The Johnny Popper was the perfect craft to take you where the big ones were biting. The manure spreader could double as a bait bucket.
(Deere & Company)

30

When the links are calling, Jack Gustafson's 1941 Allis-Chalmers WF
makes the ideal caddy cart, complete with umbrella.
(Photograph © Andrew Morland)

Space Probe

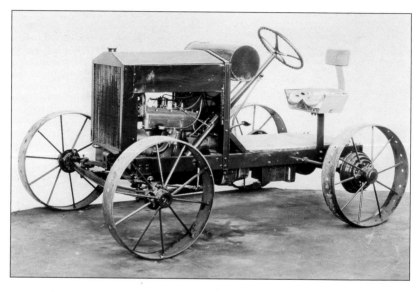

Forget $50 hammers and $200 toilet seats! This 1931 Ford-based Doodle-Bug could be the perfect lunar exploration vehicle for the space program on a budget. (Minnesota Historical Society)

When you want to ride in style, nothing impresses like the family's steam tractor. Ma or Pa make a good chauffeur. (Photograph © Jerry Irwin)

Ferrari

The 1937 McCormick-Deering O-12 Orchard shared its color scheme and swoopy styling with the exotic Italian sports car. At speed, Ferraris and IH orchard machines could sometimes be confused, even by old-timers. (Photograph © Andrew Morland)

Porsche

Curvaceous bodywork was the rule for the 1955 Case 400 Orchard and the German Porsche sports car. (Photograph © Andrew Morland)

35

Land Speed Recordsetter

Eighty-eight miles in a mere five hours and one minute? With rubber tires on your Allis-Chalmers, who knew what record would be broken next! The one thing you could be sure of is that goggles were essential to keep the bugs out of your eyes. (Minnesota Historical Society)

36

On your mark, get set, crawl! International Harvester's lineup of T-4, T-5, and TD-5 crawlers were the perfect "racers" for a slowest-moving vehicle dash.

Demolition Derby

Rather than let the old combine rust away in a back pasture, enter it in the local combine demolition derbies. These derbies offered the perfect outlet for a farmer's frustrations for every time the combine broke down. This contest of agricultural gladiators took place at the Minnesota State Fair in the 1970s before a crowded grandstand. (Minnesota Historical Society)

38

Fitted with a Ford Flathead V-8 engine, Palmer Fossum's 1952 Funk-Ford 8N was a hot-rodder's dream come true. (Photograph © Andrew Morland)

Drag Racer

With its big rear wheel and powerful 20/40 V-8 engine, the 1915 Common Sense tractor from Minneapolis, Minnesota, could beat many a tractor in a drag race to the fenceline.

This steamer could roll over any obstacle put in front of it and crush the opposition just like Big Foot.

James Bond 007 Secret Agent Vehicle

The Minneapolis-Moline UDLX boasted the latest gadgets for all
debonaire secret agents of the farmyard. (Minnesota Historical Society)

The slippery lines and low-flying capability of Dan Buckert's 1947 Case VAO Orchard help it elude radar. (Photograph © Andrew Morland)

43

UFO

The John Deere 3020 Orchard was easily mistaken for an unidentified flying object in low light, such as when it returned from work at dusk. This may have given rise to many rumored alien sightings.

44

Hang Glider

With a good wind underneath its overhead wing, the Ford 861
Powermaster could soar forever. (Photograph © Andrew Morland)

45

Fashion Accessory

Nothing made a fashion statement for the well-dressed farmer like the new John Deere Model A with Roll-O-Matic front end.

For When You're All Dressed Up But Have Nowhere to Go

You've got on your best Sunday suit and bowler hat but have nowhere to strut your stuff. . . . Might as well plow the back forty.
(Minnesota Historical Society)

47

Square Dancing

The Farmall Fast-Hitch Square Dance Kids toured North America performing their mechanized versions of the tried-and-true hoe-down at state and county fairs everywhere. The quartet of Farmall 200 tractors "danced" their repertoire of twenty basic square dance "steps." If this didn't sell you on the fleet-footedness and tight turning circle of the Farmall, nothing would.

Arrayed in front of the Minneapolis, Minnesota, factory, a lineup of
1937 Twin City tractors gets ready to strut their stuff.
(Minnesota Historical Society)

Lawn Chair

When the day is done, the hood of your John Deere is a fine place to put your feet up.

La-Z-Boy

Might as well make yourself comfortable when you have long hours ahead of you in the field. (Photograph © J. C. Allen & Son)

Poolside Lounge Chair

Nothing was better for cooling off after a long day in the tractor's seat than a dunk in the watering trough. And when you were done swimming, your tractor made an ideal deck chair for soaking up the sun's rays. (Photograph © J. C. Allen & Son)

52

Some folks see an old tractor as the ideal lawn ornament. Others view it as nothing but fertilizer, rusting back into the earth from which it came.
(Photograph © Keith Baum)

Planter

A retired John Deere boasts many benefits as a tree planter, helping your seedlings grow straight and true. (Photograph © Andy Kraushaar)

Guard
Dog

With its bulldog stance, a 1952 Ford 8N will keep burglars away. (Photograph © Andrew Morland)

A Place to Stop and Smell the Roses

Far from the hectic pace of life, there are few places better to stop and smell the roses — or at least to contemplate the dandelions — than a retired tractor. (Photograph © Andy Kraushaar)

57

Salt Lick

For some reason, Bossie always seems to like the taste of an old tractor. And after a lick or two, your favorite machine serves double duty as a backscratch. (Photograph © Andrew Morland)

58

The mammoth wheels of a John Deere articulated four-wheel-drive
tractor make an ideal spot for a nap—or bunkhouse when
unexpected guests come to call.

In the days before RVs and mobile homes were mass-produced, home-made homes-away-from-home had to be jury-rigged by creative and far-sighted inventors. This "mobile home" filled the bill in the 1910s by using a Holt crawler for power. (Glenbow Archives)

Firewood Hauler

To keep the farmhouse nice and warm in the winter months, best stock up
on some extra-large logs with the help of a Daniel Best steam tractor.

Paul Bunyan would have been most pleased with this C. L. Best
Model 60 and its load of wood.

Magic Tricks

Before your very eyes, Allen Martin's 1935 John Deere Model B will
transform into the Incredible Shrinking Farm Tractor!
(Photograph © Keith Baum)

Tanning Booth

Who needs one of those newfangled, artificial tanning booths when you have a John Deere Model A? (Deere & Company)

65

Wet Bar

Nothing builds a mighty thirst in a farmer like long hours in a tractor seat
watching the plow to make certain the furrow is running straight and true.
(Photograph © J. C. Allen & Son)

66

You could always let the crew know when it was time for a break with a steam tractor, such as this troop of Northwest machines from Stillwater, Minnesota. (Photograph by John Runk/Minnesota Historical Society)

Moonshine Still

When crop prices hit rock bottom, there were always other—
perhaps slightly dubious—ventures that could be taken on
with your handy steam tractor.

Air Traffic Controller

In the early days of air travel, navigation was aided by a friendly wave from the John Deere "ground crew" working the fields. (Deere & Company)

69

Posse

Saddled up to set off in pursuit of a dangerous desperado, there was no terrain that could stop this posse of Caterpillars. (Glenbow Archives)

70

After many long hours on the road in the station wagon en route to Disneyland or Wall Drug, this family was eager to check out a fascinating International 706 Hi-Clear, making it an ideal roadside rest stop.

Sleigh

With a trio of oxen to pull your Universal kerosene tractor over hill and dale, everyone was in high spirits to sing a rousing chorus of "Jingle Bells."

Wrapped in Christmas lights, an International 1586 is a stirring sight at Yuletide. (Photograph © Paul Rezendes)

Christmas Card

A MERRY CHRISTMAS AND HAPPY NEW YEAR

HAULING WHEAT BY MODERN METHODS.

What better way to greet old friends and let them know what's up with you and yours at Christmas time! "Hauling wheat by modern methods" down here on the farm. (Minnesota Historical Society)

74

Santa Claus always had an inkling of what you wanted under the tree.

Ice Sculpture

The family's old 1952 Ford 8N never looked more beautiful than when it was covered in ice and icicles during the winter months. You could even pull up a chair and just gaze at it. (Photograph © Paul Rezendes)

The streamlined fenders of Larry Maasdam's 1930s Caterpillar Model Twenty-Two Orchard made it look as though this Cat was designed to tend the ice. (Photograph © Andrew Morland)

A steam tractor belted up to a threshing machine always seemed to attract a crowd. (Glenbow Archives)

Emergency Repair Vehicle

The John Deere D was always willing to take a break in its work so you could help out Soapbox Derby contestant in distress. (Deere & Company)

Soapbox Derby Racer

Archaeological Excavation

To some folk, the rusting hulks of a pair of Farmalls get the heart racing.
To others, they start hands wringing: One person's treasure is another's
junk. (Photograph © Andrew Morland)

Junk Pile Starter Kit

Step Ladder

DELTA MODEL

Tractor Stilts

4½ Ft. Clearance
6 Ft. Clearance

*For literature and prices
contact*
**The Tractor-Stilts Co., Inc.
7205 Lawndale Dr.
Omaha, Nebraska**

The Tractor Stilts conversion for your Ford 8N made it an ideal step ladder. Finally, just one farmer was needed to change a light bulb.

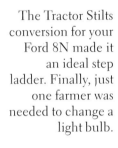

84

Photo Opportunity

The Johnny Popper was a part of the family and appeared in many a
family portrait. (Deere & Company)

Plowing and seeding in spring offered plenty of feed for the birds, and whether you appreciated the sight or not, a tractor seat often made a fine perch for bird watching.

For Making Hay While the Sun Shines

Allis-Chalmers's WC was a tractor the whole family could enjoy.

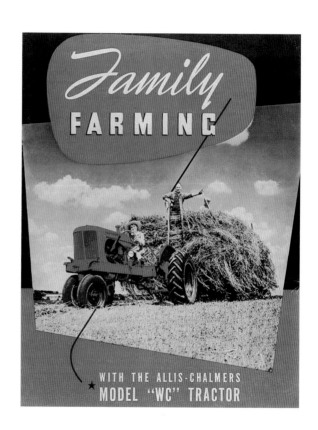

Family **FARMING**

WITH THE ALLIS-CHALMERS
MODEL "WC" TRACTOR

Shade at the End of a Long, Hot Day

The bigger the tractor, the more shade it threw—something that was always appreciated during lunchtime or at the end of the day.

For Being Pretty in Pink

For some tractor buffs, pink is the color of choice, as with this Farmall H. (Photograph © Andy Kraushaar)

89

Conversation Piece

John Deere's new Diesel Model R was the conversation topic on many farmsteads.

90

Bragging Rights

Who wouldn't want to brag about their brand-new Massey-Harris?

Who needs to buy a Harley-Davidson or take up playing the saxophone
when you could sit proudly on your Farmall H?

Room With a View

Corner office? Office with a window? The view from the tractor seat was usually the best one around. (Photograph © Jerry Irwin)

93

Everyone knows that farmers—with help from their trusty Farmalls—
have green thumbs.

Joy Ride

Other folks have sports cars or muscle cars, but for farmers, the new
Ferguson puts the biggest smile on your face.

95

Memory Book

Many stories could be told about the olden days and the marvels of the John Deere Model D. (Deere & Company)

Barn Support

Old barns often seemed pleased to have a tractor underneath them for support. (Photograph © Keith Baum)

97

Many old farmers were also happy to have that tractor underneath them.

98

One of the Ties That Bind

The Johnny Popper was just one of the good things about the farming life. (Deere & Company)

Faithful Steed to Ride
Off into the Sunset

The sun sets behind an old farmer
and an old tractor still going strong.
(Photograph © Jerry Irwin)

100

Happy Ending

An old tractor
provided a happy
ending to many
a day.

101